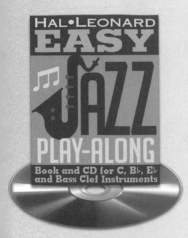

Hal • Leonard

EASY JAZZ

Easy Jazz
PLAY-ALONG

Book and CD for C, B♭, E♭
and Bass Clef Instruments

EASY JAZZ CLASSICS

HAL•LEONARD
EASY JAZZ PLAY-ALONG
Book and CD for C, Bb, Eb
and Bass Clef Instruments

EASY JAZZ CLASSICS

Volume 3

18 Classics
for Beginning Jazz Musicians

Recorded by Ric Probst at Tanner Monagle Studio
Piano: Mark Davis
Bass: Tom McGirr
Drums: Dave Bayles

ISBN 978-1-4584-1517-2

HAL•LEONARD®
CORPORATION
7777 W. BLUEMOUND RD. P.O. BOX 13819 MILWAUKEE, WI 53213

Visit Hal Leonard Online at
www.halleonard.com

CONTENTS

BOOK

CONTENTS

CD

Afternoon in Paris

C Version

BY JOHN LEWIS

DOXY

C VERSION

BY SONNY ROLLINS

500 MILES HIGH

C VERSION

WORDS BY NEVILLE POTTER
MUSIC BY CHICK COREA

2ND TIME RIT.

Girl Talk

FROM THE PARAMOUNT PICTURE HARLOW

BY NEAL HEFTI

C VERSION

HOLY LAND

C VERSION

BY CEDAR WALTON

IMPRESSIONS

C VERSION

BY JOHN COLTRANE

14

IN WALKED BUD

C VERSION

BY THELONIOUS MONK

THE JIVE SAMBA

C Version

By Nat Adderley

LADY BIRD

C VERSION

BY TADD DAMERON

MERCY, MERCY, MERCY

C VERSION

COMPOSED BY
JOSEF ZAWINUL

RIT. (LAST TIME)

MY LITTLE SUEDE SHOES

C VERSION

BY CHARLIE PARKER

RECORDA-ME

C VERSION

BY JOE HENDERSON

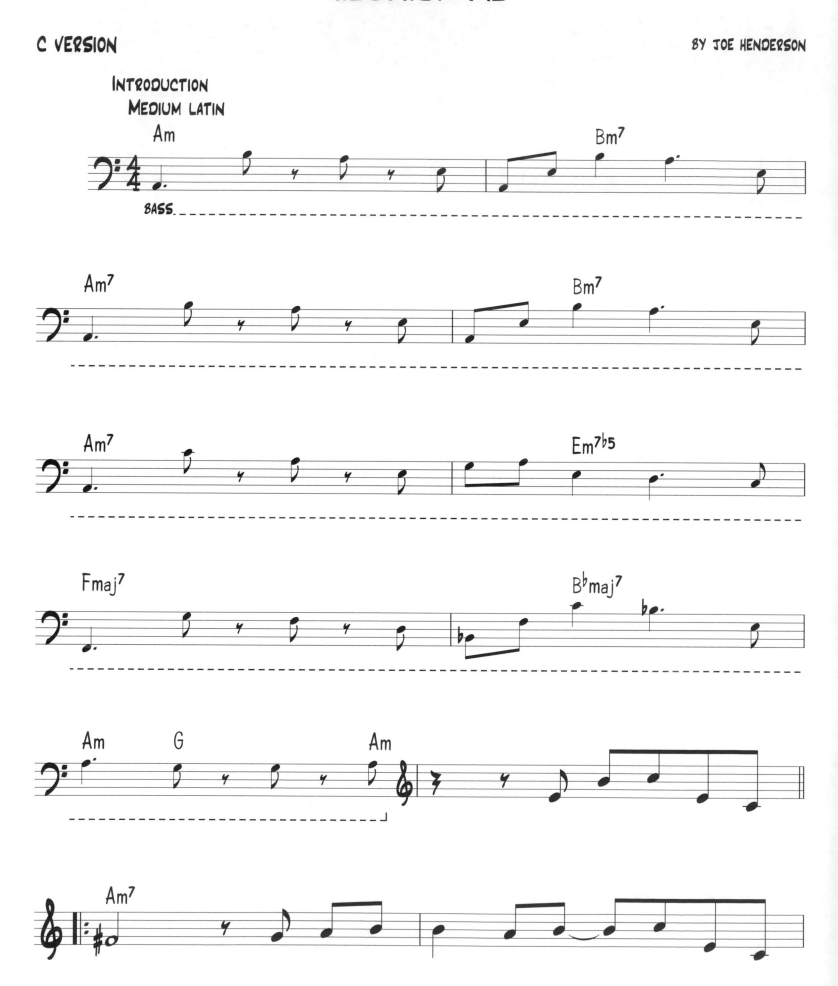

St. Thomas

C Version

By Sonny Rollins

SIDEWINDER

C VERSION

BY LEE MORGAN

SOLAR

C VERSION

BY MILES DAVIS

STOLEN MOMENTS

C VERSION

WORDS AND MUSIC BY
OLIVER NELSON

INTRODUCTION
MEDIUM SWING

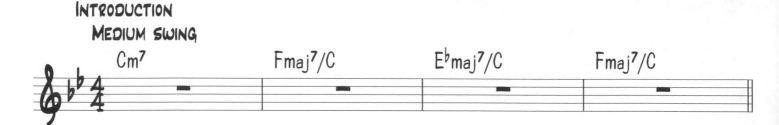

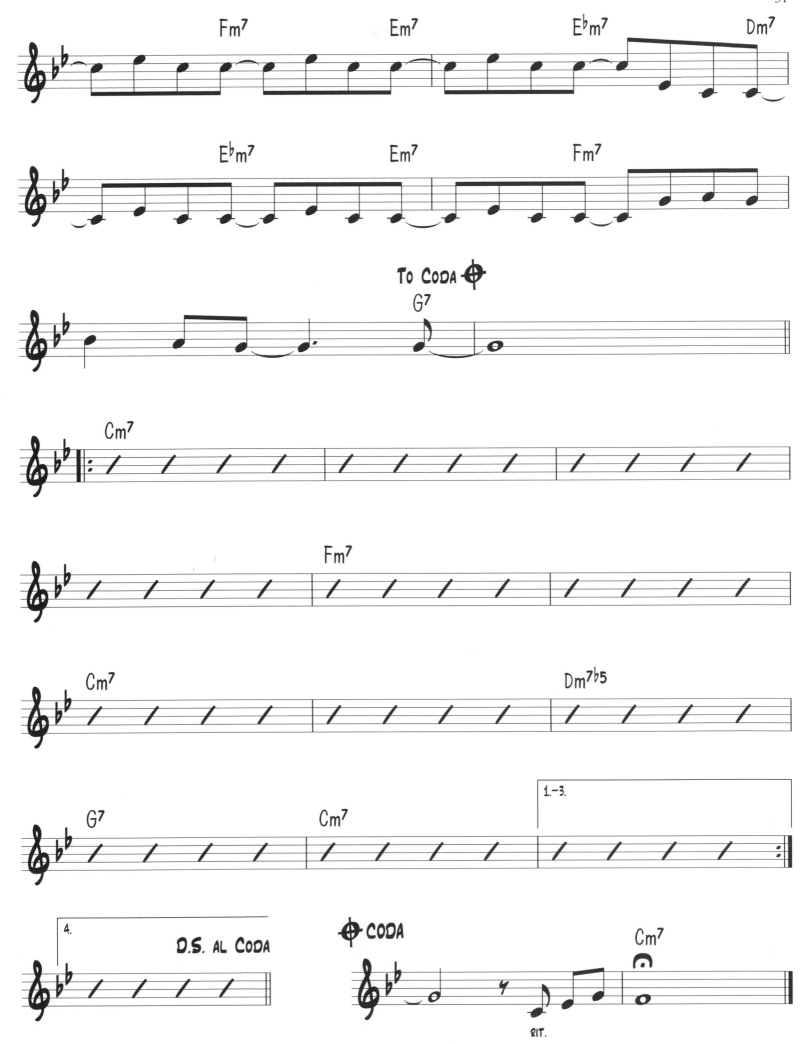

Sunny

C Version

WORDS AND MUSIC BY
BOBBY HEBB

INTRODUCTION
MEDIUM 12/8 FEEL

THINK ON ME

C VERSION

By George Cables

Afternoon in Paris

Bb Version

By John Lewis

Doxy

Bb Version

BY SONNY ROLLINS

SOLOS

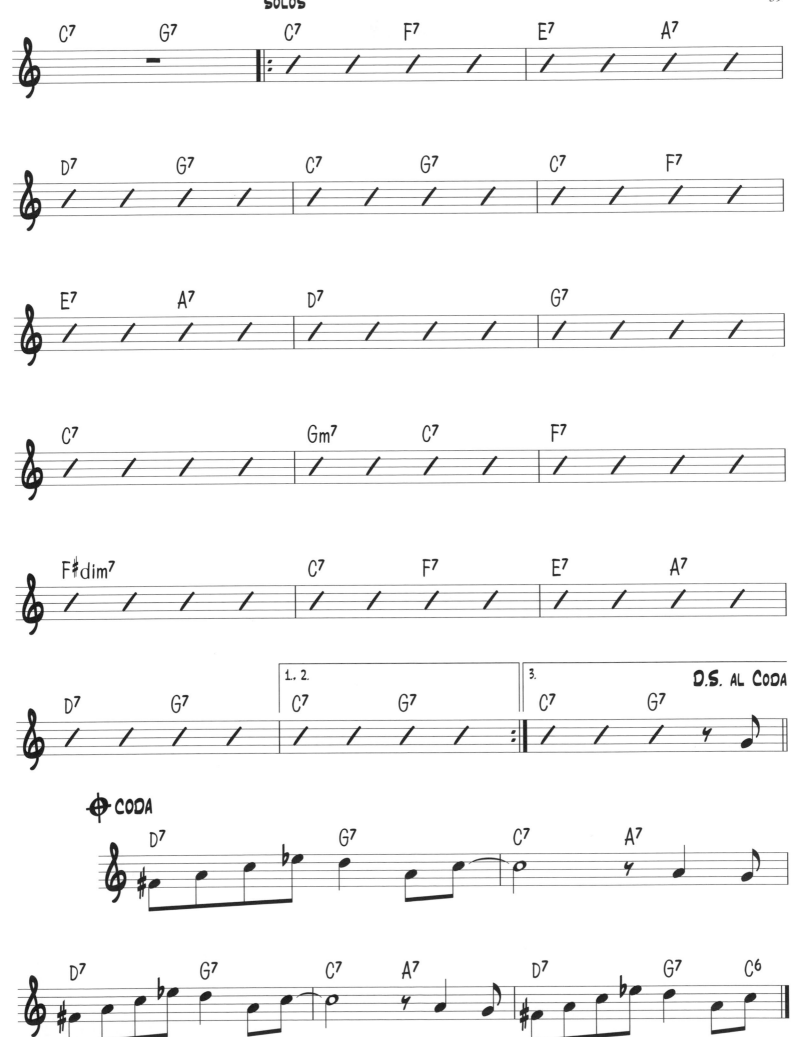

500 MILES HIGH

Bb VERSION

WORDS BY NEVILLE POTTER
MUSIC BY CHICK COREA

2ND TIME RIT.

Girl Talk

FROM THE PARAMOUNT PICTURE HARLOW

BY NEAL HEFTI

Bb VERSION

HOLY LAND

Bb VERSION

BY CEDAR WALTON

IMPRESSIONS

BY JOHN COLTRANE

Bb VERSION

IN WALKED BUD

Bb Version

BY THELONIOUS MONK

THE JIVE SAMBA

Bb VERSION

BY NAT ADDERLEY

LADY BIRD

Bb VERSION

BY TADD DAMERON

MERCY, MERCY, MERCY

COMPOSED BY
JOSEF ZAWINUL

Bb VERSION

INTRODUCTION
SLOW FUNKY ROCK

RIT. (LAST TIME)

MY LITTLE SUEDE SHOES

Bb VERSION

BY CHARLIE PARKER

RECORDA-ME

Bb VERSION

BY JOE HENDERSON

ST. THOMAS

Bb VERSION

BY SONNY ROLLINS

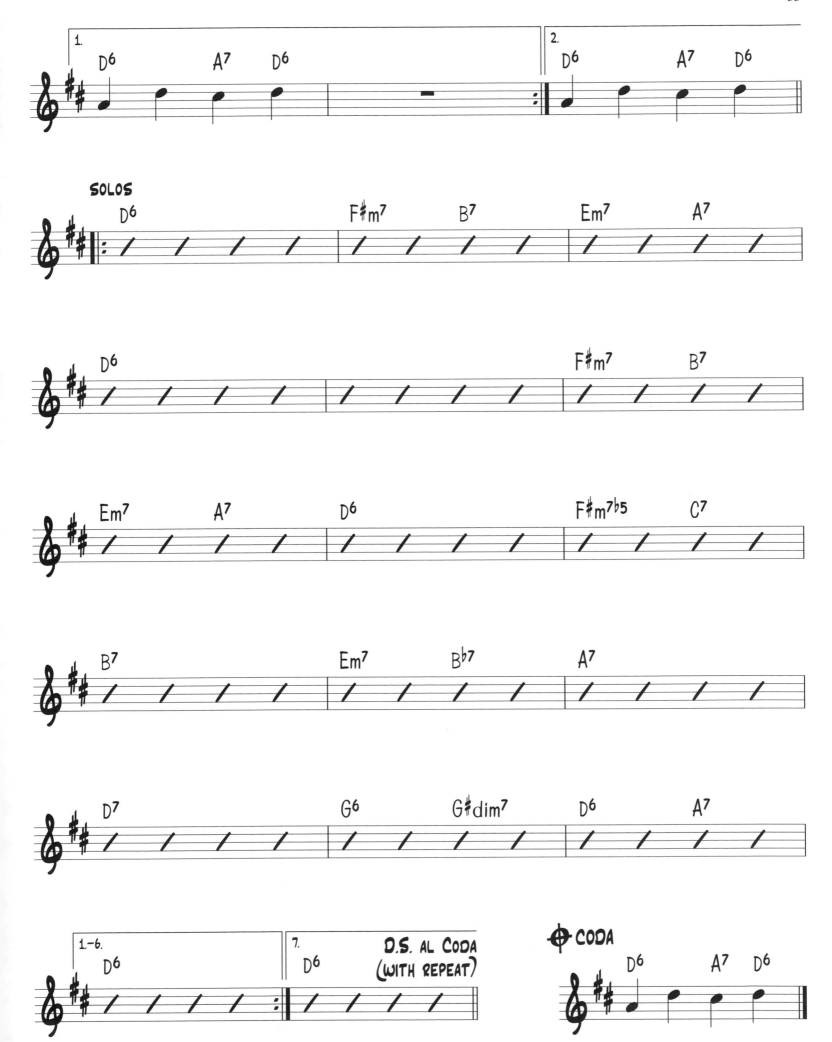

Sidewinder

Bb Version

By Lee Morgan

SOLAR

Bb VERSION

By Miles Davis

STOLEN MOMENTS

Bb Version

Words and Music by
Oliver Nelson

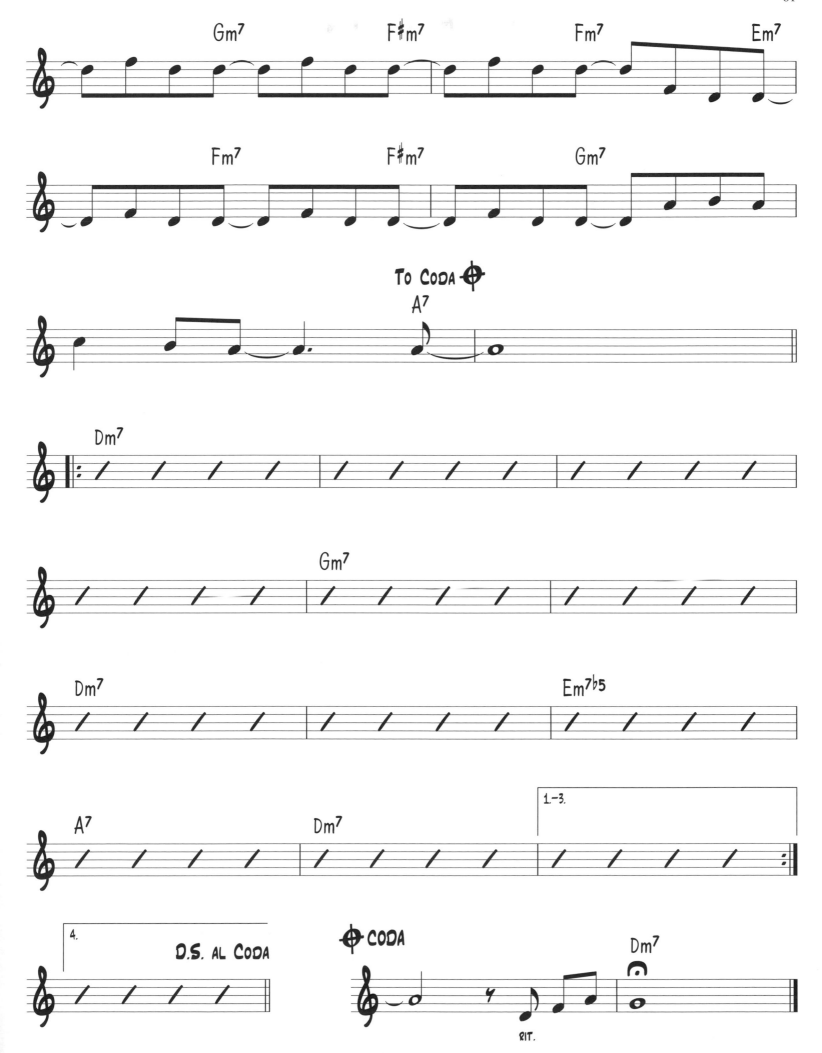

Sunny

Bb Version

WORDS AND MUSIC BY
BOBBY HEBB

Introduction
Medium 12/8 feel

THINK ON ME

Bb VERSION

BY GEORGE CABLES

65

AFTERNOON IN PARIS

Eb Version

By John Lewis

Doxy

Eb Version

By Sonny Rollins

SOLOS

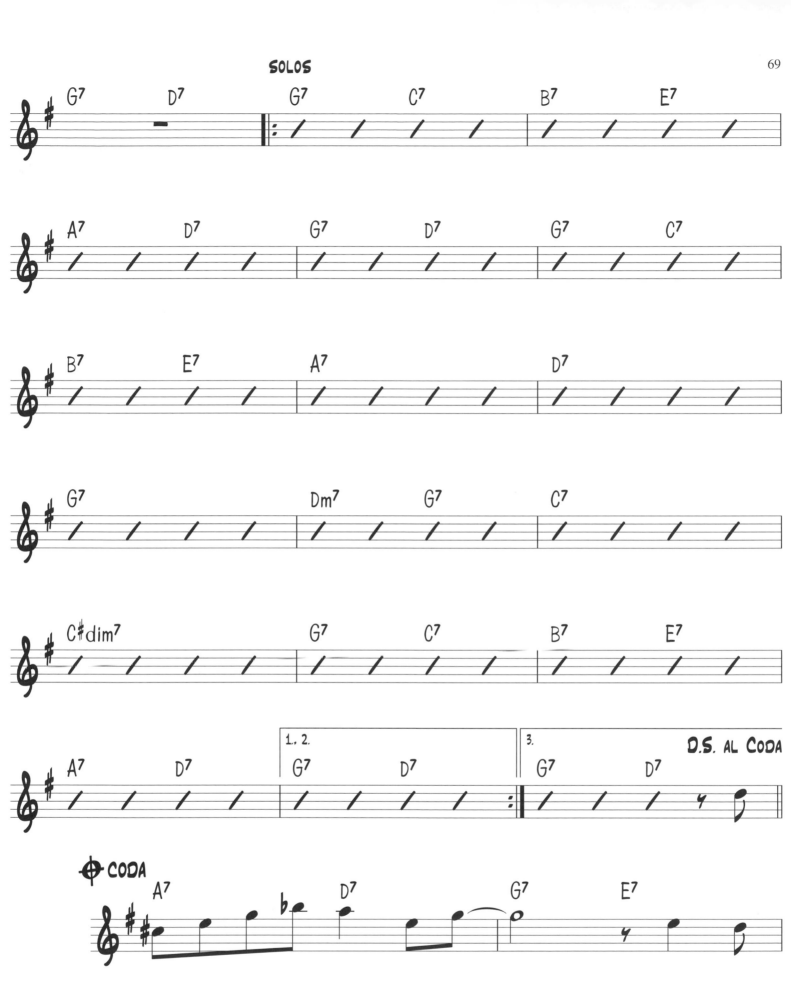

500 MILES HIGH

Eb VERSION

WORDS BY NEVILLE POTTER
MUSIC BY CHICK COREA

2ND TIME RIT.

GIRL TALK

FROM THE PARAMOUNT PICTURE HARLOW

BY NEAL HEFTI

Eb Version

HOLY LAND

Eb VERSION

BY CEDAR WALTON

IMPRESSIONS

BY JOHN COLTRANE

Eb VERSION

In Walked Bud

Eb Version

By Thelonious Monk

THE JIVE SAMBA

Eb VERSION

BY NAT ADDERLEY

LADY BIRD

Eb VERSION

BY TADD DAMERON

Mercy, Mercy, Mercy

Eb Version

COMPOSED BY
JOSEF ZAWINUL

INTRODUCTION
SLOW FUNKY ROCK

RIT. (LAST TIME)

My Little Suede Shoes

By Charlie Parker

Eb Version

RECORDA-ME

Eb VERSION

BY JOE HENDERSON

ST. THOMAS

Eb VERSION

BY SONNY ROLLINS

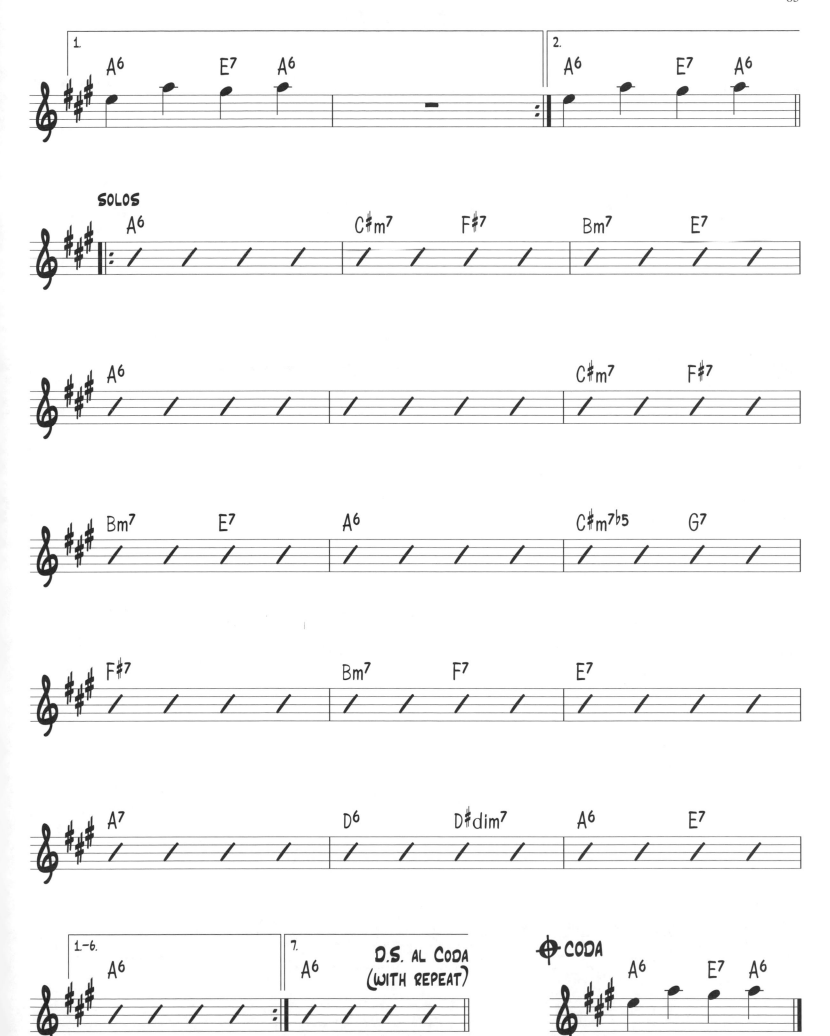

Sidewinder

Eb Version

By Lee Morgan

SOLAR

Eb Version

BY MILES DAVIS

STOLEN MOMENTS

Eb Version

WORDS AND MUSIC BY
OLIVER NELSON

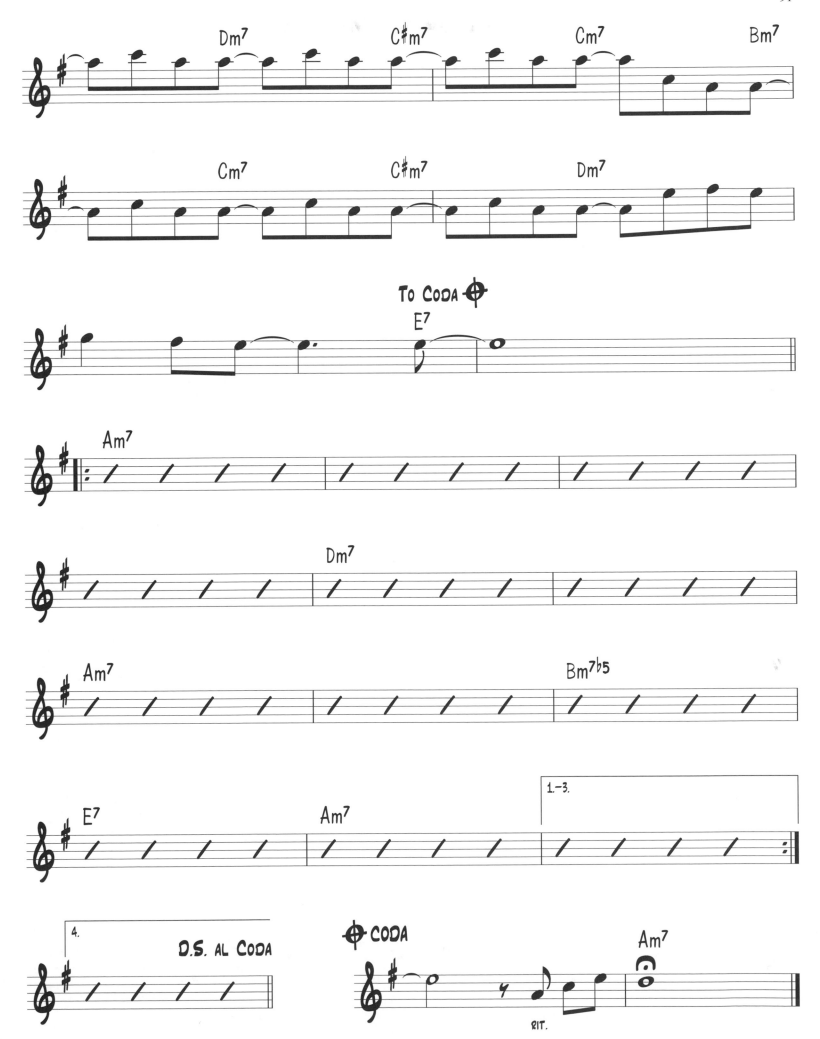

Sunny

WORDS AND MUSIC BY
BOBBY HEBB

Eb Version

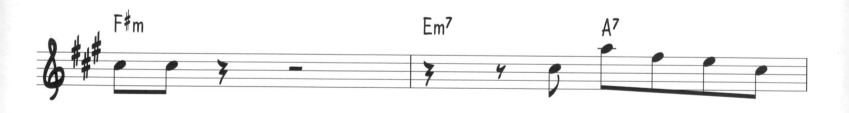

Think on Me

By George Cables

Eb Version

AFTERNOON IN PARIS

Doxy

𝄢 C Version

By Sonny Rollins

SOLOS

500 Miles High

: C Version

Words by Neville Potter
Music by Chick Corea

2nd time rit.

Girl Talk

FROM THE PARAMOUNT PICTURE HARLOW

C VERSION

BY NEAL HEFTI

HOLY LAND

🎵 C VERSION

BY CEDAR WALTON

IMPRESSIONS

BY JOHN COLTRANE

C VERSION

IN WALKED BUD

𝄢 C Version

BY THELONIOUS MONK

THE JIVE SAMBA

C Version

BY NAT ADDERLEY

LADY BIRD

𝄢: C VERSION

BY TADD DAMERON

RIT.

MERCY, MERCY, MERCY

: C VERSION

COMPOSED BY
JOSEF ZAWINUL

RIT. (LAST TIME)

MY LITTLE SUEDE SHOES

C Version

BY CHARLIE PARKER

RECORDA-ME

𝄢 C VERSION

By Joe Henderson

INTRODUCTION
MEDIUM LATIN

St. Thomas

9: C Version

By Sonny Rollins

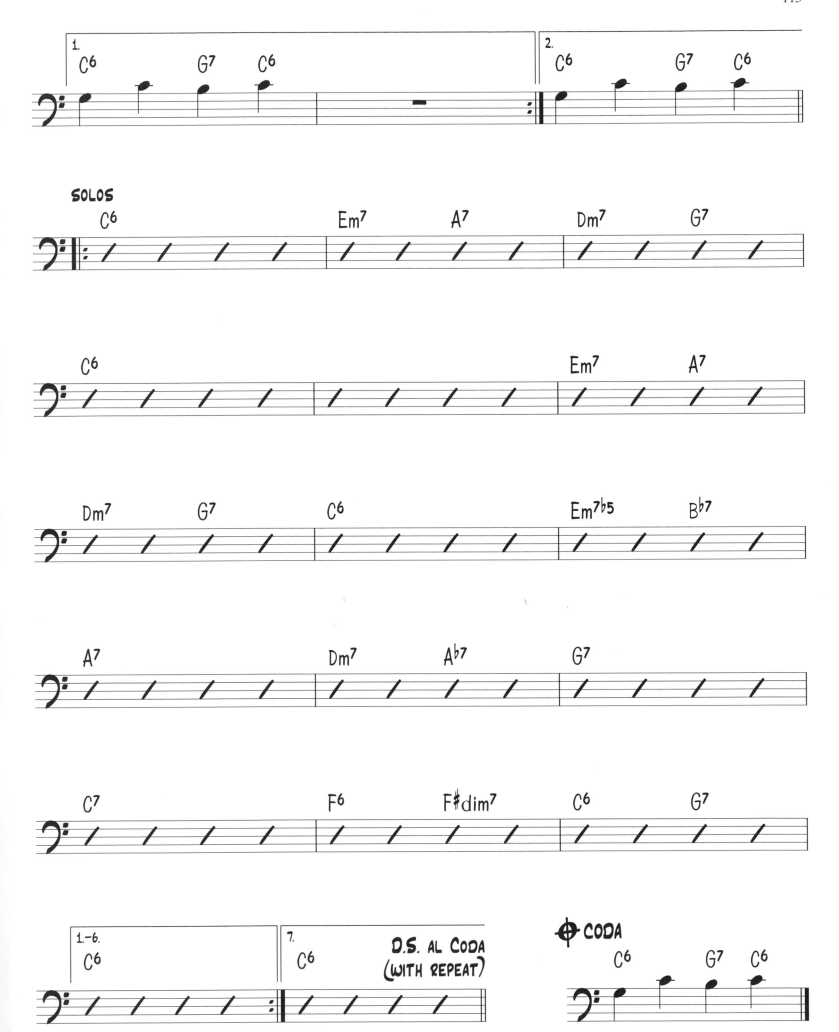

Sidewinder

‿: C Version

BY LEE MORGAN

SOLAR

𝄢 C VERSION

BY MILES DAVIS

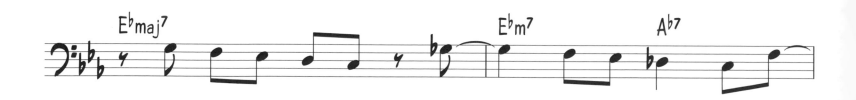

STOLEN MOMENTS

Words and Music by
Oliver Nelson

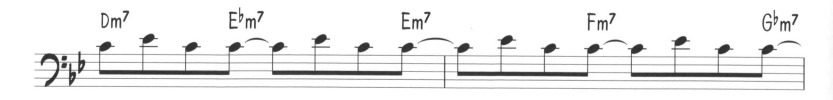

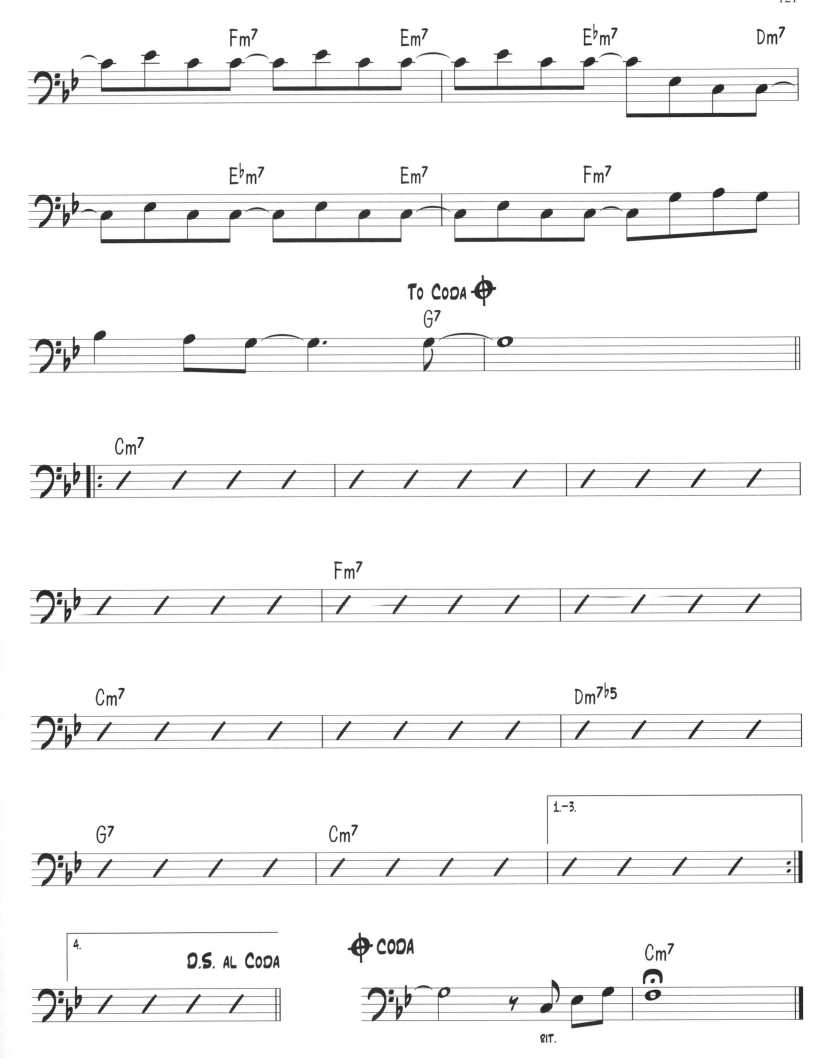

Sunny

𝄢 C Version

WORDS AND MUSIC BY
BOBBY HEBB

Think On Me

C Version

BY GEORGE CABLES

MEDIUM JAZZ ROCK

Presenting the Hal Leonard JAZZ PLAY-ALONG® SERIES

For use with all B-flat, E-flat, Bass Clef and C instruments, the Jazz Play-Along® Series is the ultimate learning tool for all jazz musicians. With musician-friendly lead sheets, melody cues, and other split-track choices on the included CD, these first-of-a-kind packages help you master improvisation while playing some of the greatest tunes of all time. FOR STUDY, each tune includes a split track with: melody cue with proper style and inflection • professional rhythm tracks • choruses for soloing • removable bass part • removable piano part. FOR PERFORMANCE, each tune also has: an additional full stereo accompaniment track (no melody) • additional choruses for soloing.

63. CLASSICAL JAZZ
00843064 ....$14.95

64. TV TUNES
00843065 ....$14.95

65. SMOOTH JAZZ
00843066 ....$16.99

66. A CHARLIE BROWN CHRISTMAS
00843067 ....$16.99

67. CHICK COREA
00843068 ....$15.95

68. CHARLES MINGUS
00843069 ....$16.95

69. CLASSIC JAZZ
00843071 ....$15.99

70. THE DOORS
00843072 ....$14.95

71. COLE PORTER CLASSICS
00843073 ....$14.95

72. CLASSIC JAZZ BALLADS
00843074 ....$15.99

73. JAZZ/BLUES
00843075 ....$14.95

74. BEST JAZZ CLASSICS
00843076 ....$15.99

75. PAUL DESMOND
00843077 ....$14.95

76. BROADWAY JAZZ BALLADS
00843078 ....$15.99

77. JAZZ ON BROADWAY
00843079 ....$15.99

78. STEELY DAN
00843070 ....$14.99

79. MILES DAVIS CLASSICS
00843081 ....$15.99

80. JIMI HENDRIX
00843083 ....$15.99

81. FRANK SINATRA – CLASSICS
00843084 ....$15.99

82. FRANK SINATRA – STANDARDS
00843085 ....$15.99

83. ANDREW LLOYD WEBBER
00843104 ....$14.95

84. BOSSA NOVA CLASSICS
00843105 ....$14.95

85. MOTOWN HITS
00843109 ....$14.95

86. BENNY GOODMAN
00843110 ....$14.95

87. DIXIELAND
00843111 ....$14.95

88. DUKE ELLINGTON FAVORITES
00843112 ....$14.95

89. IRVING BERLIN FAVORITES
00843113 ....$14.95

90. THELONIOUS MONK CLASSICS
00841262 ....$16.99

91.THELONIOUS MONK FAVORITES
00841263 ....$16.99

92. LEONARD BERNSTEIN
00450134 ....$15.99

93. DISNEY FAVORITES
00843142 ....$14.99

94. RAY
00843143 ....$14.99

95. JAZZ AT THE LOUNGE
00843144 ....V$14.99

96. LATIN JAZZ STANDARDS
00843145 ....$14.99

97. MAYBE I'M AMAZED★
00843148 ....$15.99

98. DAVE FRISHBERG
00843149 ....$15.99

99. SWINGING STANDARDS
00843150 ....$14.99

100. LOUIS ARMSTRONG
00740423 ....$15.99

101. BUD POWELL
00843152 ....$14.99

102. JAZZ POP
00843153 ....$14.99

**103. ON GREEN DOLPHIN STREET
& OTHER JAZZ CLASSICS**
00843154 ....$14.99

104. ELTON JOHN
00843155 ....$14.99

105. SOULFUL JAZZ
00843151 ....$15.99

106. SLO' JAZZ
00843117 ....$14.99

107. MOTOWN CLASSICS
00843116 ....$14.99

108. JAZZ WALTZ
00843159 ....$15.99

109. OSCAR PETERSON
00843160 ....$16.99

110. JUST STANDARDS
00843161 ....$15.99

111. COOL CHRISTMAS
00843162 ....$15.99

112. PAQUITO D'RIVERA – LATIN JAZZ★
48020662 ....$16.99

113. PAQUITO D'RIVERA – BRAZILIAN JAZZ★
48020663 ....$19.99

114. MODERN JAZZ QUARTET FAVORITES
00843163 ....$15.99

115. THE SOUND OF MUSIC
00843164 ....$15.99

116. JACO PASTORIUS
00843165 ....$15.99

117. ANTONIO CARLOS JOBIM – MORE HITS
00843166 ....$15.99

118. BIG JAZZ STANDARDS COLLECTION
00843167 ....$27.50

119. JELLY ROLL MORTON
00843168 ....$15.99

120. J.S. BACH
00843169 ....$15.99

121. DJANGO REINHARDT
00843170 ....$15.99

122. PAUL SIMON
00843182 ....$16.99

123. BACHARACH & DAVID
00843185 ....$15.99

124. JAZZ-ROCK HORN HITS
00843186 ....$15.99

126. COUNT BASIE CLASSICS
00843157 ....$15.99

127. CHUCK MANGIONE
00843188 ....$15.99

132. STAN GETZ ESSENTIALS
00843193 ....$15.99

133. STAN GETZ FAVORITES
00843194 ....$15.99

134. NURSERY RHYMES★
00843196 ....$17.99

135. JEFF BECK
00843197 ....$15.99

136. NAT ADDERLEY
00843198 ....$15.99

137. WES MONTGOMERY
00843199 ....$15.99

138. FREDDIE HUBBARD
00843200 ....$15.99

139. JULIAN "CANNONBALL" ADDERLEY
00843201 ....$15.99

141. BILL EVANS STANDARDS
00843156 ....$15.99

150. JAZZ IMPROV BASICS
00843195 ....$19.99

151. MODERN JAZZ QUARTET CLASSICS
00843209 ....$15.99

157. HYMNS
00843217 ....$15.99

162. BIG CHRISTMAS COLLECTION
00843221 ....$24.99

★These CDs do not include split tracks.

IMPROVISING IS EASIER THAN EVER

with this new series for beginning jazz musicians. The Hal Leonard Easy Jazz Play-Along Series includes songs with accessible chord changes and features recordings with novice-friendly tempos. Just follow the streamlined lead sheets in the book and play along with the professionally recorded backing tracks on the CD. The bass or piano can also be removed by turning down the volume on the left or right channel. The audio CD is playable on any CD player. For PC and Mac computer users, the CD is enhanced so you can adjust the recording to any tempo without changing pitch!

1. FIRST JAZZ SONGS
Book/CD Pack

All of Me • All the Things You Are • Autumn Leaves • C-Jam Blues • Comin' Home Baby • Footprints • The Girl from Ipanema (Garôta De Ipanema) • Killer Joe • Little Sunflower • Milestones • Mr. P.C. • On Green Dolphin Street • One for Daddy-O • Reunion Blues • Satin Doll • There Will Never Be Another You • Tune Up • Watermelon Man.

00843225 Bb, Eb, C & Bass Clef Instruments............... $19.99

3. VITAL JAZZ CLASSICS
Book/CD Pack

Afternoon in Paris • Doxy • 500 Miles High • Girl Talk • Holy Land • Impressions • In Walked Bud • The Jive Samba • Lady Bird • Maiden Voyage • Mercy, Mercy, Mercy • My Little Suede Shoes • Recorda-Me • St. Thomas • Solar • Song for My Father • Stolen Moments • Sunny.

00843227 Bb, Eb, C & Bass Clef Instruments............... $19.99

2. STANDARDS FOR STARTERS
Book/CD Pack

Don't Get Around Much Anymore • Exactly like You • Fly Me to the Moon (In Other Words) • Have You Met Miss Jones? • Honeysuckle Rose • I Remember You • If I Should Lose You • It Could Happen to You • Moon River • My Favorite Things • On a Slow Boat to China • Out of Nowhere • Softly As in a Morning Sunrise • Speak Low • The Very Thought of You • Watch What Happens • The Way You Look Tonight • Yesterdays.

00843226 Bb, Eb, C & Bass Clef Instruments............... $19.99

4. BASIC BLUES
Book/CD Pack

All Blues • Birk's Works • Bloomdido • Blue Seven • Blue Train (Blue Trane) • Blues in the Closet • Cousin Mary • Freddie Freeloader • The Jody Grind • Jumpin' with Symphony Sid • Nostalgia in Times Square • Now See How You Are • Now's the Time • Sonnymoon for Two • Tenor Madness • Things Ain't What They Used to Be • Turnaround • Two Degrees East, Three Degrees West.

00843228 Bb, Eb, C & Bass Clef Instruments............... $19.99

HAL•LEONARD® CORPORATION

7777 W. BLUEMOUND RD. P.O. BOX 13819 MILWAUKEE, WI 53213

Prices, content, and availability subject to change without notice.